For Winifred,

The best mom that

A girl could ever ask for

July 14, 2014

When the lights go out
Your heart may too.
I don't know when you'll go.
That's my greatest fear.

When a hero dies,
Everyone mourns.
When you die,
How do I know I won't too?
That's my greatest fear.

Your body is deteriorating.
I can't bear to let you go.
Who's going to be there
When I fall apart?
That's my greatest fear.

I tell you I love you
Over and over again.
I can't stand the thought
Of you not hearing those last words.
That's my greatest fear.

I'm getting well just for you.
But when you're gone,
There's no one else to fill that place.

Then there's no point anymore.

That's my greatest fear.

I want to make you proud,

But, how can I?

I already feel like I've failed you.

How do I continue life without you?

That's my greatest fear.

<u>Introduction</u>

I think everyone can agree that they dislike Mondays. I know I do. It used to be because I had to wake up early for a round of classes that I probably wasn't ready for due to procrastination. But now I don't just dislike Mondays, I hate them. July 11 was supposed to be a good day. For the most part it was. My mom was in the hospital and she was supposed to be out today, but doctors decided that she needed a few more days. They decided by the end of the week she will be home. Anybody who knows me could tell you how much I loved my mother. Our bond was like peanut butter and jelly. We just went together. On this particular Monday though, it was a hot day but not too hot. I was bored and lonely. I had gone to the library and took out nine books. My mother would have had my head because I knew she limited me to three books due to all the fines I rack up sometimes. I stayed at the library till closing, which was around 6 pm. When I left, I took out my phone and called her like any other time. The phone rang a few times and as it was ringing, I kept repeating in my head "please pick up" because I really wanted to talk to her. Eventually she did pick up. She didn't sound too good. I could tell she was on the nebulizer for her asthma. I could tell she was having trouble breathing. But I put all of that aside because I was just happy to hear her voice. I ask her how she is and she says she has some pain in her chest. I tell her I miss her and I can't wait to see her when she gets home. I bring up my boyfriend to her as I always do when I'm feeling insecure. I ask her if she is sure he will write me. She tells me yes. I ask her if she is sure that he loves me. And she says yes. As we are talking, I hear in the background someone coming into her room. It sounds like a woman. It's probably a nurse. My mom says something back to the person and tells me that she has to go and that she will call me back later. With that we tell each other "I love you" and hang up.

My mom has been yapping at me for a few months now to help her clean her room. She even said she would pay me a hundred dollars to do it. The thing is I have cleaned her room a few times in the past and each time I cleaned it the room would eventually go back to how it was, full of clutter and piles as high as the ceiling. This Monday though, I decided to clean her room so I could surprise her when she gets home.

Here's how it went, I walked into her room and I started in the corner under her window next to her bed. It just seemed like the ideal place to start. I stripped the room down. I got rid of the ants that crawled on her nightstand. I got rid of soiled tissues, empty candy wrappers, empty wine bottles and a bunch of paper. I had plenty of garbage bags. I put her clean clothes on her bed and the dirty ones in the hallway to be taken down to be washed. The amount of dust in the room would make anyone feel like they were dying of allergies. I cleaned the top of her dressers. Put things in order and made it look pretty. At this point you could see the whole floor from the bedroom door to the corner where I started. It was wonderful to see how much progress I had made. And as I was going through clothes, I heard the phone ringing downstairs. I ran downstairs and grabbed the first phone I could reach, saw the caller ID, and it said Beth Israel. That was the name of the hospital my mother was staying at. When I picked up, there was no one on the other end. They had already hung up. I went back upstairs and I texted my sister, Jennifer, who was at our sister Joyce's house down the block. "Beth Israel called the house. Isn't that the hospital mom's at?" I ask her. A few minutes later she calls and asks what the hospital wanted. I say I didn't get to the phone in time. She asks me to go into the kitchen and look up the number from which the hospital called and I tell her. She tells me she is going to call the hospital back and see what was up. I made my way back into my mother's room. I sat on this red stool that she had kept in the corner that I had started cleaning from. I had moved it when I was cleaning and now, I was sitting on it. I was starting to panic. My chest was getting tight, I felt like I couldn't breathe. I knew something was wrong because why would the hospital call the house at 11pm. I had called my best friend knowing very well she was at work. My best friend picked up the phone and I told her that the hospital called and I was worried. While I was on the phone, I went into a panic attack. My best friend told me I was going to be fine; my mother was going to be fine, and that she was going to be home at the end of the week like the doctors said. I felt a bit calmer after that. But now I was feeling like I was annoying my best friend. I could hear her yelling at someone she was working with. I told my best friend I would talk later. Nothing felt right at all. I felt a heaviness take over me. A piece of me felt like I was dying. I had a gut feeling that something bad was happening. And my gut is always right.

It didn't seem to fail me this time when the house phone rang again. I ran downstairs, saw that it was my sister, and picked it up immediately. "It's mom. She's not well. Get Nathaniel ready. We're going to pick you up." With that, I hung up the phone. I was panicking on the inside. I felt like everything around me was collapsing. I ran upstairs and told my brother to get shoes on because we had to go to the hospital; mom is not doing well. Within five or so minutes my sister's car pulled up and we jumped in and rushed to the hospital. During the drive all I felt was dread. I put a brave face on and told myself I wouldn't cry. I need to be strong.

Walking into the hospital I felt numb. There was no one to truly prepare me for what I was about to see. We walked down the white halls, passing nurses, doctors, other families, but not a smile in sight. How could you smile in a place like this? There was no happiness. We finally found her room. I walked in. There she was, my mother, the one who raised me, the one who loved me. I barely recognized her. She wasn't conscious. We couldn't talk. There was all this brown stuff all over her. Her hair was sweaty. Her dignity, gone. I had no words while I loomed over her head. I had no tears. I was empty. I knew she was gone. I felt her leave when I was in her bedroom.

The doctors said they were going to try and get her to ICU that night. They said they were just waiting on a bed. My family and I just stood around. There wasn't much we could do. My sisters were crying. I understood but I couldn't let myself cry. Other family members came and checked up on each other. At some point people went home because we were all waiting for her to be moved. I refused to go home. I wasn't going to miss the chance of seeing her wake up or miss the chance of saying goodbye. Going home wasn't an option for me. Around 3am doctors had gone into her room. A moment later, some young doctor who looked like he belonged in California surfing came out of the room. He walked up to us and said, "I'm so sorry." Those dreaded words. How could he possibly be sorry? He had no idea. A moment ago, they said they were moving her to the ICU and a moment later they're saying sorry. How pathetic. That was a joke. A big joke. I went into the room again. I looked down at her. I put my hand on her forehead and wiped some of her hair away. I whispered in her ear, "I love you mom." I took a picture of her. Just like that she was gone. I blamed the hospital. I blamed the doctors. I could not cry at this moment. My best friend, my peanut butter, my mom, my whole world just left me. It didn't feel real. I did not sleep. From the moment she passed away to the funeral, I did not cry. I put this strong façade on and kept telling myself, "She's in a better place now. I shouldn't be selfish." Truth was, I was angry at her for leaving me and never explaining to me how I was supposed to survive without her.

Letter 1

Mom,
I'm glad I said goodbye,
said, " I love you" one last time.

Letter 2

Late nights

can't sleep

getting tired

clock strikes 3.

Morning it is

guilt trips me

anger fuels me.

You're gone

wasn't ready

Took a part of me.

Left alone

feels like rotting.

wasting away

wishing for you.

Energy drained

people suck

Can't keep up

What's the point?

Wasn't ready

wasn't prepped

left without warning

now regret hits

Three words

wasn't enough

you're gone

I'm here

wasn't fair.

Greatest fear

now it's here

<u>Letter 3</u>

Down the hall I stare

Into what seems like an abyss.

Beyond the darkness

Lies your bedroom

The sight of it is chilling,

Freezes me where I stand.

I know you aren't there,

Yet I still deny the truth.

Walking into darkness

It's quite a tale you see.

I've been there before

With you by my side.

Never thought I'd come again

Without you here.

Chills go down my spine,

Chest gets tighter,

Tears start forming,

And still, you don't appear.

Facts are right in front of me.

Doesn't stop me though.

I still walk down that dark hall

And push open your bedroom doors

To say hello

In hopes you'll return it

Throughout the room,

Throughout the darkness,

Throughout the house

There's only silence.

And that's what broke my heart.

<u>Letter 4</u>

Alone,

Rotting in this house.

As I sit in silence

Behind closed doors

I can hear the floors creak.

No one's home but me.

Is it you mom?

Are you out there?

Is this all just a joke

And you've finally come back home?

I walk to your room again

And open up the doors.

Even though I can see

That you aren't there

I still say, "Hello? Mom?"

I hear my voice crack.

Tears start forming

And I wonder why I even bother.

Letter 5

Despair no longer lingers here.

Hate has left my heart.

When I look towards the sky,

A sea of color

Ripples through the clouds.

I know you're there

Watching over me.

Love has never been stronger.

I forgot it was there.

But when I look up

I know you're there.

I feel you lingering.

When I walk down the street

I feel you next to me.

When I feel like I'm going insane,

I know you're there to ease my mind.

I've tried not to think of you,

But you were my first true love.

You showed me love

When I thought I was unlovable

You taught me how to love

When I had such a bitter heart.

I can't repay you for what you gave me,

But I can make you proud.

I still cry when I think of you.

The memories are vivid like a dream.

I hated you,

But I'm learning to love you again.

I'm crazy for what I want,

But you would have wanted me to go after it.

I still feel lonely with you gone,

But your voice message

With an "I love you"

Makes me feel like you're still here.

I can't keep wishing

About things that I can't control.

Because the fact is

You're not coming back.

But I can live for you.

I can keep my promise to you,

"Gabby, Live your life."

<u>Letter 6</u>

Since You've been gone
I've lost who I am.

I don't know where to go

Or where to turn to.

I lost my best friend,

My security,

My support,

Most importantly my mom.

You left

And I fell apart.

I'm broken down into pieces.

I don't believe in myself anymore.

I have little faith.

I don't know what I'm doing anymore.

<u>Letter 7</u>

I'm not sure how I'm supposed to feel,

But I can tell you it's nothing good.

Back at it again

With the same old thoughts.

Maybe they never went away.

Maybe I never got better.

It's possible I just got comfortable.

It's possible I got used to it all,

And just let it all become a part of me.

The fact is I sit here

Thinking the same thoughts,

The same thoughts

That occurred years ago.

Wasn't therapy supposed to be a cure?

Weren't the pills supposed to be a cure?

And what about all the hospital visits?

Shouldn't I be cured by now?

Shouldn't I be happy and healthy?

I thought that,

But I guess I'm wrong.

Maybe this is who I am.

Maybe I never changed.

Maybe I just got used to all the pain.

It's possible her passing

Was a stressor

For it all to come back again.

Maybe It's her fault this is who I am.

I just want to know why.

Why do I feel this way?

Why am I not better?

Why do I still want to die?

Why don't I believe in myself?

Why do I feel so lost?

I try to have some normalcy in my life,

But what's normal?

Because I'm not it

I'm the definition of a person

Sitting on the line

Between sanity and insanity.

Letter 8

Another night

Drowning in tidal waves

Of my own tears.

The only friend

Sitting next to me

Is the darkness that consumes me.

They say I keep it all to myself

But if you felt as alone as I do

Then you probably would too.

Went from being on cloud nine

With my crown sitting high,

Now I'm below the surface

With water all around me

Filling up my lungs.

Do you know what suffocation feels like?

There's nothing romantic about it.

It's violent,

Gasping for air that isn't there.

My lungs explode

Like a balloon when it hits a needle.

Needles aren't so bad though.

Maybe if I had one

I could have a moment,

A blissful moment.

Forget about everything

Just for a few minutes

Maybe I'd see your face again.

The way your wrinkles

Crinkled by your eyes

When you smiled.

Maybe a hopeful touch.

Just one more hug.

Let me hear your voice again.

Tell me you love me one last time

Because this voice message

Doesn't cut it anymore.

They say I have everything,

But truly I have nothing.

I lost it all when you left,

And people just don't understand it.

A roof over my head,

Clothes on my back,

And food on the table.

It's all great and dandy

Don't get me wrong,

I'm not being selfish.

But I would give it all up

If it meant I could be with you again.

Constantly,

I hear your advice

Rolling around in my head,

But it's not the same.

You were the strong one

For the both of us.

I guess this what they mean

By survival of the fittest

Because you should be here,

And I don't think I can survive this on my own.

Letter 9

Think you have to die

to go to heaven?

I'm sitting in it

And I'm not dead.

Not physically,

But when half your soul is dead

I suppose heaven

Is a place to be freely traveled to.

The only sad part

Is the sky separates us

From the loved ones

We came to see.

What's the point

Of being able to go back

And forth from heaven

If you can't see your loved one?

Maybe it's the view

Or the feeling of being closer,

But heaven's right in front of me,

And I feel you near me.

Maybe that's good enough.

<u>Letter 10</u>

Crashing and burning

Like a car crash on the side of the road.

I'm losing it.

Put in front of a judge and jury

I'd probably plead insanity.

The anger inside me

Is like a wildfire.

One I can no longer contain.

Why am I breaking my back

Just to make ends meet?

I know what I want.

I know how to get there.

Constantly I'm falling

And I'm about to call it quits.

Don't know how much

More I can take.

People call themselves my friends

But when I need a friend

There's no one in sight.

That's because friends

No longer exists in my world.

I'm alone to fend for myself.

It's me against the world,

And it's always been that way.

Never believe you have anyone

Because they'll prove you right.

You have no one.

I'm angry

And no one understands it.

I'm emotional

And all they say is suck it up.

I'm done hiding my feelings.

I'm done playing this game.

I'm breaking all the rules

And I don't care about consequences.

Letter 11

Nervous mess

Arms shaking

Heart beating faster.

Think I'm going crazy.

Mom I wish

You were here.

I feel like I'm messing up.

I don't know what I'm doing.

Please help me.

Please help me.

Letter 12

You never truly stop crying.

Middle of night

And the tears just pour,

Creating an ocean.

When the heart breaks it howls,

Turns tears into a tsunami.

Not a day goes by

When I don't think of you,

When I'm not reminded of you.

Mom,

You don't understand.

The days go by slower.

My heart fills with anger.

I'm not sure if I'm breaking

Or becoming someone else.

Lately,

I don't recognize myself.

Cold hearted,

Anger filled,

Breaking ties,

Becoming reckless.

Forward is not my direction.

Backwards is not where I'm at.

I'm somewhere in the middle.

People are complaining

Of who I'm becoming

But I'm so distant

I don't care.

Others support the change,

Say I've grown mature

And I know what I want.

Few say I'm lost

And I'm not going to make it,

But they're all telling lies.

The only person I want to hear is you.

I just want to hear you

Tell me I'm not crazy,

Tell me I'll make it,

Tell me you believe in me.

Mom,

I'm losing hope,

Losing faith.

I feel lost in my own mind.

People just don't understand.

I lost my best friend.

Screw all the people

That call themselves my best friend

Because you've always

Been my number one.

I lost the one person

Who truly understood me,

Who put up with me,

Who loved me

No matter how badly I messed up.

I lost the walls

That surrounded my kingdom.

I feel like

I'm losing this battle.

I can't deny

I have days

Where I know you're there.

I'm living my life

For the both of us now.

You won't see me graduate college,

But I'll make it

As far as I can go.

You won't see me get married,

But I'll live by your principles.

You won't see me have children,

But I'll teach them

Everything you ever taught me.

At the end of the day

I'll make you proud.

I owe that to you.

Maybe this is too much to ask,

But just watch over me.

<u>Letter 13</u>

It's 2am

Just like every other

Night this week.

I'm awake

And crying,

But nobody hears me.

I doubt anyone cares.

It always starts

With a late-night walk

To the bathroom.

I always look down

The hall towards your room.

It hits me every night

The overwhelming emotion

Of you not being here.

I miss you.

My tears get heavier

And I wish I had

Someone who understood,

Understood my pain.

Mom,

No one understands me

Like you did.

Letter 14

Ever since you left,

Slipped away forever,

I've been doubting myself.

I don't know if I can

Do this without you.

I try to stay put together

But constantly fall apart.

I don't have anyone

But me to put myself back together.

Let's be honest mom,

You were my rock.

You were the walls

That held me high.

Now I'm nothing.

It's nights like these

That I feel like joining you.

All I want

Is for you to hold me,

Tell me I'll be okay.

I can't deal with my thoughts anymore.

I wish they'd stop,

At least for a moment.

I wasn't ready

To let you go.

I wasn't prepared

When you slipped away.

You left me here

Broken and bruised.

No one can help me.

No one understands me.

Sometimes I feel like

Dying is the only answer.

Why should people stop me?

It's not like I matter.

When you left

You took more of me

Then I could bear.

I'm not whole.

I'm shattered

And I don't know

How to put myself

Back together again.

I don't want to

Feel like this forever.

<u>Letter 15</u>

House on the hill

Treating you all the time.

Making you proud of me.

That's all I ever wanted.

You saved me from a life that would have destroyed me.

But I couldn't save you.

I feel like I didn't fight hard enough.

I knew you needed to go to the hospital.

I should have pushed harder.

I should have done more.

But you were just so stubborn.

That night when you fell was the worst.

I didn't know what to do.

That week was hell.

I knew you weren't alright.

I knew something was wrong.

But no one listened to me,

Not even you.

I could have saved you,

I should have pushed harder.

You stopped taking care of yourself,

Your health declined to the worst it ever had

been.

You stopped caring.

Stayed in your room for hours.

I knew I was losing you

And yet I let you convince me that you were

alright.

And you finally went to the hospital

I thought we were all good.

You were going to get better.

The doctor said you were coming home.

But that night, alone in your room,

I knew you were gone.

No one will ever understand

What I felt that night.

I felt you leave.

And I felt you take a huge chunk of me.

And since then,

I've been angry,

Lonely.

I've hated you for leaving me.
And nights like these,

Tonight,

Where I've had too much to drink,

I can't help but miss you.

I don't know who I am without you.

<u>Letter 16</u>

Lonelier than ever,

It's just one of those nights.

I'm thinking about you

And your last days here.

I was stupid.

All I talked about was him.

You were dying

And I called you every day

For your last week here

To have you reassure me

That he loved me.

What I should have done

Was tell you

How much I love you.

That you needed to stay

Because I needed you.

Now here I sit

At the hour of 2am

Alone

In my room

Crying for you to be here.

Memories of us flashing

Through my mind.

I can hear your voice

And it breaks my heart.

I got my chance to say

I love you

One last time,

I just hope

You were able to hear it.

Tonight's rough.

I miss you

With every fiber in me.

I want you to be proud of me,

But I also want to be with you.

I'm torn between the two.